deborah alun-jones & john ayton

charming

the magic of charm jewelry

with 108 illustrations, 102 in color

Thames & Hudson

First published in 2005 in hardcover in the
United States of America by Thames & Hudson Inc.,
500 Fifth Avenue, New York, New York 10110

thamesandhudsonusa.com

Library of Congress Catalog Card Number
2004111175

ISBN-13: 978-0-500-51213-5
ISBN-10: 0-500-51213-2

Picture research: Mariana Sonnenberg

Printed and bound in Singapore by
Star Standard Industries

contents

the charm
of a charm

'Cocktail jewelry ... is about martinis, furs, fast cars and Monte Carlo. It evokes images of Marilyn Monroe.'

Geoffrey Munn of the jeweler Wartski

Charms are the fashion sensation of the day, but their history is long and their future assured. For, whether affordable or priceless, specially commissioned or vintage, whimsical or mystical, charms weave spells that appeal to our most primeval desires. The guises they take may vary, but the needs they fulfil are as old as time. These magical pieces of jewelry offer us love, luck and protection – themes that have endured through the centuries and across the continents.

All the great jewelers of the world have always made charms but, in our hectic and challenging world, jewelry has become more personal and meaningful than ever. Charms reflect the personality of their wearer and, in so doing, offer us a *band of identity*. Today's examples can take any form, from an exotic claw, tooth or piece of stone, as worn by the actor Orlando Bloom, to delicate vintage lovebirds, to the fabulous high-heeled shoe that all girls covet.

Collections of individual charms tell the *story of a lifetime*. One of Elizabeth Taylor's first pieces of jewelry was her charm bracelet, and she has added to it year on year. It is this personal significance that gives the charm a special resonance for every wearer.

Many of us also have personal stories of the *romance of charms* – a mother whose bracelet started with a single heart given to her by her husband on their wedding day, and added to by him ever since: an intricately worked tortoise as a souvenir of a trip, a lifebelt to remember the launch of a ship, a tiny lawnmower as a memento of the first marital home.

As a treasury of memories, charms mark the passage of time in an unforgettable way. They commemorate high days and holidays, and act as mementoes of the important things in our lives – birthdays and weddings, friendships and love affairs, *pastimes and passions*. When Frank Sinatra gave Marlene Dietrich a bracelet of poker chips, he was celebrating their shared love of gambling.

As Sinatra's gift shows, charms have been crafted in an astonishing range of materials, including jade, coral and animal horn, rhinestones, sterling silver and gold. It is not surprising that countless stylish women have succumbed to their allure. Famed fashion designers Coco Chanel and Elsa Schiaparelli were both champions of the charm bracelet. Likewise these bracelets have long adorned the wrists of Hollywood royalty. When Grace Kelly appeared in the 1954 film *Rear Window* wearing one, a fashion craze was born.

Though brace
incarnation, c
different ways
Anna Sui's ca
handbag, tuck
ring, a cell-ph
much-loved p
becomes a bra
from its minia
as the *way*
celebrate our

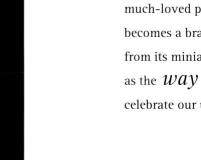

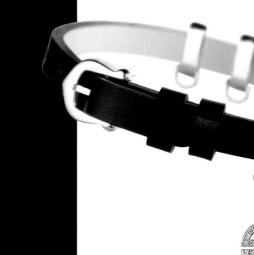

In the eighteenth century our fashion-conscious forebears combined practicality and style in the *châtelaine*, or équipage. Domestic trinketry such as miniature keys, seals, and even tweezers and folding scissors were suspended on chains and hooked via a decorative panel onto the wearer's waist. Bijoux pieces could be added over time, making each châtelaine a fashionable and unique expression of its owner.

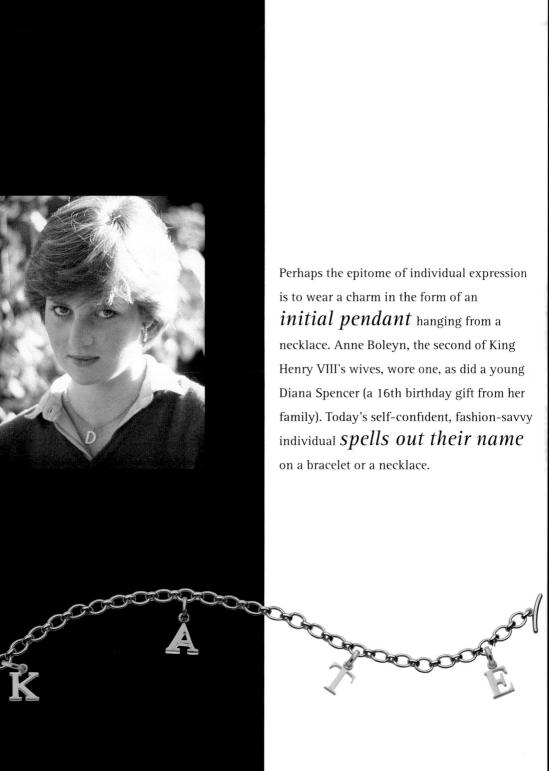

Perhaps the epitome of individual expression
is to wear a charm in the form of an
initial pendant hanging from a
necklace. Anne Boleyn, the second of King
Henry VIII's wives, wore one, as did a young
Diana Spencer (a 16th birthday gift from her
family). Today's self-confident, fashion-savvy
individual *spells out their name*
on a bracelet or a necklace.

The whole history of charms is bound up with the history of jewelry. One of the earliest pieces of jewelry, *the cowrie shell,* was worn 20,000 years ago as a charm to enhance fertility and avert the Evil Eye. The shell features on this Ancient Egyptian string of amulets of gold and semi-precious stones, and is still used to provide protection and comfort today.

When Bear Grylls, the youngest man to climb Mount Everest, embarked on his momentous expedition, he took a cowrie shell with him. He and his wife Shara had found it on a beach, and she had it inscribed with a message: 'Be sure of this, that I am with you always, even unto the ends of the earth' (Matthew 28: 20). When Bear was at 26,000 feet and frightened, the cowrie shell offered him a sense of protection beyond price. In surrounding ourselves with our own particular treasures in the shape of charms, we feel safe and loved.

This is the charm of charms. They can be whatever we want them to be, from a pebble discovered on a deserted shore to the most exquisite diamond pavé heart. Some of us are drawn to charms through personal inspiration, others by a love of their whimsy and sense of fun, still others by a fascination with their ancient and magical roots. Now, as charms enjoy a remarkable twenty-first-century renaissance, this anthology tells their story.

chapter 1 •
magical
talismans

'While Vogue *was considering all the little vanities that make life worth looking at, it realized that the struggle was of no avail unless one possessed a talisman...*'

Vogue, *November 1916*

Whatever name we give to these delicate pieces of jewelry – talismans, lucky charms, touchstones – their allure is as strong today as it was for our spellbound ancestors.

In ancient cultures the Evil Eye posed a very real danger. With one glance, death and destruction could be visited on the unfortunate individual, so a myriad different forces were brought into play to repel the Eye. The cowrie shell offered protection 10,000 years ago, and still in Azerbaijan today *blue 'eye'* charms are attached to babies' underclothing to avert the Eye's malevolent gaze.

For the Ancient Egyptians, the scarab was one of the most powerful of amulets, and it has been in continuous use since 4,000 BC. *The scarab*, or dung beetle, was believed to represent the sun's movement across the sky and therefore became the symbol of the life force itself. It was also believed to hold the power to ensure rebirth in the afterlife – the Ancient Egyptians' main spiritual preoccupation – because the beetles' young would emerge from holes in the ground as if the adults had been 'reborn'.

The journey the Ancient Egyptians undertook to the afterlife was fraught with danger, so personal protective measures were needed. *Tutankhamen's gold mask* was adorned with a representation of a cobra, one of the young pharaoh's heraldic creatures.

When, during archaeological digs in Victorian times, charms began to emerge alongside ancient treasures, jewelry designers such as Fortunato Castellani and his sons took up the passion for these symbols, and Egyptian motifs began to appear in abundance.

In John Galliano's Spring/Summer 2004 haute couture collection for Christian Dior, the *magical power* of the scarab was used to combine an ancient protective motif with stunning modern glamour.

Cartier have also drawn on ancient *symbols of protection*, such as the turtle, in their charm collections. In Eastern belief systems the turtle and its landlocked cousin deity, the tortoise, are seen as supporting the cosmos and have come to symbolize eternal life, wisdom and strength. As a protective amulet the tortoise has long been worn to bring wisdom and to avert sudden death. Tortoiseshell charms are also worn as a defence against black magic.

Charms always played a part in the cultural lives of ancient communities. They were worn by all levels of Roman society, from gladiators to emperors. Hadrian had a talismanic ring in the form of an inscribed topaz, and he believed that this brought him success in battle, as topaz was known as the stone of strength.

For Roman boys, before they got near the battlefield, surviving childhood was a feat in itself, and the protection of a charm was required. These boys were given a *bulla* at their naming ceremony, nine days after birth. Bullae were large pendants, made of gold or a less precious material depending on the wealth and status of the boy, and they contained protective amulets. The youth would wear the bulla as a lucky charm until the day he became a citizen, and sometimes afterwards if he met with success in later life and needed protection from the envy of others.

With the advent of Christianity, such charms became more decorative than amuletic, but the Christians, or Copts, of Upper Egypt still tied bullae containing dust made from saints' bones or other sacred relics around the necks of their dead.

Early pilgrims wore badges to protect them on their journeys to and from holy shrines. In Chaucer's *Canterbury Tales* the yeoman has 'a crystoffe' on his breast. St Christopher, from the Greek *Christoporos*, meaning Christ-bearer, has been used as a protective device for travellers since the third century. His image was particularly popular in the Middle Ages.

The *St Christopher* is still favoured as a protective comfort for travellers today. In the early days of motor travel, a popular extra supplied by Dunhill was a piece of dashboard furniture embossed with a St Christopher image and the words 'Go Your Way in Safety'.

When the crusaders of the twelfth and thirteenth centuries embarked on long and hazardous journeys from Europe to the Holy Land, they were accompanied on their way by the divine protection of the cross, which they wore emblazoned on their shields and tabards. The word 'crusade' comes from the Spanish *cruzada*, meaning 'marked with a cross'. The Garrard Knightrider collection, under the creative direction of Jade Jagger, draws from these ancient chivalric roots and from *heraldic emblems* of protection.

The ladybird is another charm with a Christian resonance. In the Middle Ages the ladybird was dedicated to Our Lady, the Virgin Mary. Still a symbol of good luck today, it is believed to bring wealth and success, and to prolong good health by absorbing disease from the wearer. Cartier's exquisite ladybird charm in white gold sports wings of diamonds with ruby spots.

Many well-known figures have relied the power of charms. *Queen Vi* was devoted to them and even adopte the custom of surrounding the body personal charm jewelry in death. Lik Tutankhamen, the queen stipulated 1 personal charms and sentimental trea to accompany her in her grave. The l included not only her own wedding r but also the wedding ring belonging mother of her faithful servant John E

Screen siren *Marlene Dietrich* was also buried with her precious travel charms. In life she had been terrified of flying. When she boarded a plane she would take out a gold chain hung with a cocktail of charms: 'one cross, one miraculous medal, one St Christopher medal, one Capricorn insignia, the Star of David – and a rabbit's foot.' Once the plane had landed, the charms would be replaced in their bag until the next flight. Dietrich tried to cover all options, with influences ranging from Christianity to the Zodiac. Her daughter Maria tells movingly of her last voyage: 'Carefully I place the small chamois bag containing her travel charms by her side. She has a long journey before her and might want them.' Much like the amulets of the Ancient Egyptians, Dietrich's charms would shield her from danger on her final passage.

Dietrich also gave charms to others. When war broke out, she presented her friend, the writer *Ernest 'Papa' Hemingu[...]* with this fine gold pendant inscribed with the words 'Think of me, Papa, and be safe[...]

Magical or miraculous charms have commonly been used in times of war, when man is at his most vulnerable and in greatest need of protection. In the Victorian era, 'Mizpah' brooches were particularly popular for lovers who were to be parted by war. Through the brooch the soldier carried with him loving protection from home, often symbolized by a heart, as well as divine protection: 'And Mizpah: for he said, The Lord watch between me and thee, when we are absent one from another' (Genesis 31: 49).

Charms offering the protective power of a loved one have continued to augment the soldier's armoury. During the First World War a small elephant with an upturned trunk dangled from the wrist of many a footsoldier. The lucky elephant may be derived from the Hindu god Ganesha, who has an elephant's head on a human body and is believed to protect the household.

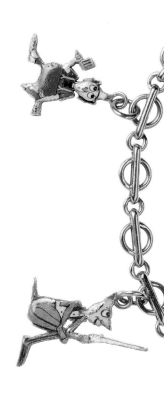

During the Second World War, mechanical or other ill luck was put down not only to the recognizable enemy, but also to mischievous elfin creatures known as gremlins. These teasing, harrying sprites were immortalized in this delightful *gremlin charm* bracelet made by Cartier, London, in 1943.

Pilots also painted their aircraft with lucky symbols, such as four-leafed clovers, to bring good fortune. Unlucky symbols, such as the number 13, were used to deflect bad luck, in the age-old belief – *similia similibus curantur* – that like would deflect like.

The 'Fumsup' figurine and the American victory bracelet from Tiffany were both made to bring comfort to men at war. In dangerous times, *solace and security* have always been derived from that most magical of things, the precious charm.

chapter 2
spiritual devotion

'They have their crystals, I do know, and rings,
And virgin parchment, and their dead man's skulls,
Their raven wings, their lights, and pentacles,
With characters; I ha' seen all these.'

Ben Jonson, The Devil is an Ass, *Act I Sc. ii*

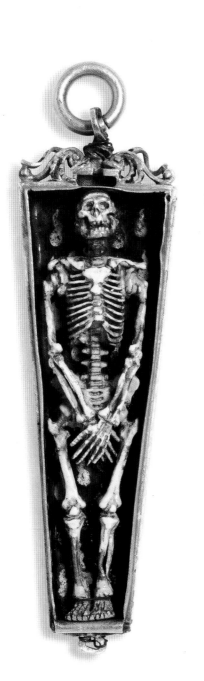

Charms have long been part of the eternal battle between Good and Evil. In the days of Early Christianity, the magical merged with the miraculous and, although the Church found it difficult to marry the notion of magic with the concept of Divine Providence, charms remained sacred. Most drew their power from the earlier pagan gods of a particular culture and era.

Memento mori, literally 'remember that you must die', were worn by the living as protection against the temptations of this world, in order to ensure acceptance in the world to come. This striking English example from 1540–50, made of gold enamelled in black and white, is inscribed with an intricate design.

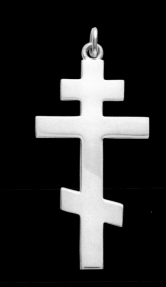

However, the most important charm in the devotional armoury is the cross. This was in use thousands of years before Christianity. Crude forms of a cross of equal lengths, known as a Greek cross, have been discovere[d] dating from as early as the fifteenth century BC. Many jewelers have been drawn to the form for its elegance, restrained simplicity and protective qualities. The *Tsar cross* from Links of London is a sleek, contempora[ry] version of the Russian Orthodox cross.

The *Maltese cross* appears as early as 800 BC. It is thought to have symbolized the heavens and has come to mean divine protection and prosperity. When Christopher Columbus arrived in America, he found the cross already incorporated into the culture of the North American Indians, where it symbolized the Tree of Life. The cross was later to become one of Coco Chanel's favourite forms of charm, reinterpreted in the 1930s by the jeweler Fulco di Verdura, a devout Catholic who was fascinated by the insignia of ancient religious orders such as the Knights of Malta.

In our own time, the eclectic lifestyle company Chrome Hearts have used the form of the *cross* inventively, in a sterling silver cut-out dog-tag pendant with pavé diamonds.

For the Bantu tribes of Africa the world is an arrangement of cross and spiral, and a cross tattooed onto the skin or onto a piece of wood symbolizes both North, South, East and West as well as the four paths crossing the universe leading to the house of Spirits, Mankind, Good Souls and Bad Souls.

Early Christians ascribed magical powers to the signing of the cross and used it to protect themselves and to declare their spiritual affiliation. The custom is thought to have gained prevalence around AD 110 and the sign was drawn on houses and chattels for divine protection.

Parts of what became known as The True Cross, believed to have been excavated in Jerusalem by the Empress Helena on 3 May AD 326, were thought to work miracles and were highly prized.

The cross, most commonly in its Latin form, has remained as the most visible of *devotional and fashionable* charms. Madonna placed it on the map as a fashion statement in the 1980s. The reappearance of the diamond cross around the swan-like necks of supermodels in the 1990s also marked a return to jewelry with a meaning drawn from historical symbolism. This charm bracelet from Theo Fennell's Outline collection shows four different depictions of the cross: Greek, Byzantine, Maltese and a Tau design.

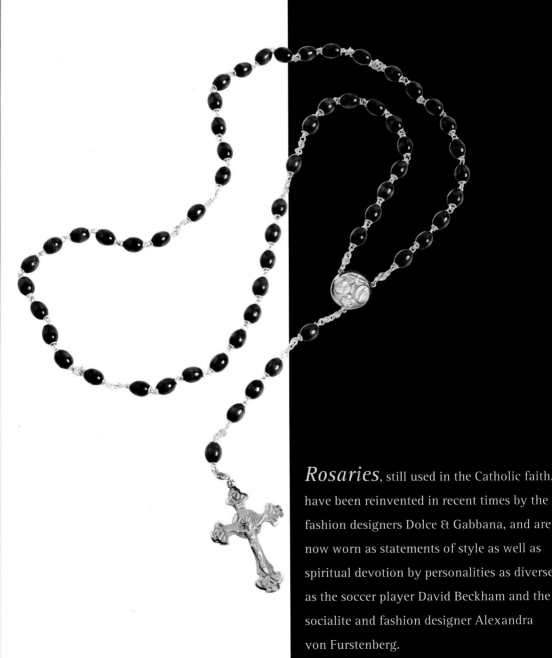

Rosaries, still used in the Catholic faith, have been reinvented in recent times by the fashion designers Dolce & Gabbana, and are now worn as statements of style as well as spiritual devotion by personalities as diverse as the soccer player David Beckham and the socialite and fashion designer Alexandra von Furstenberg.

Other traditional Christian symbols have long been used to offer protection and to cure ills. *Inscribed coins*, worn for their talismanic qualities as early as the Cassite period (14th century BC), were used centuries later by British sovereigns to cure the King's Evil, or scrofula. The royal 'touch' involved the monarch personally hanging a coin decorated with the image of St Michael around the neck of a sick person. When production of the coins ended in the seventeenth century, models were made especially for the ceremony, as can be seen in the touch-piece worn by Dr Samuel Johnson, reputed to have been the last person in England to be 'touched' by a sovereign. Coco Chanel, meanwhile, used a dramatic mix of gilt coins and more contemporary pieces to unique effect.

Episodes from the Bible, such as the story of Noah's Ark and the giving of the Ten Commandments, have also been the subject of ingenious charm bracelets. Combining *heavenly protection* and human endeavour, they echo the finely wrought memento mori of earlier centuries, worn to protect the wearer from earthly temptation.

Symbols from the East have also travelled the trade routes of thought to the West, where they have been readily adopted by a world hungry for jewelry with a magical or spiritual resonance. *The Laughing Buddha*, a symbol of happiness, kindness and innocent joy, has become one of the most popular of charms, and is the inspiration for Links of London's 'Good Charma' collection.

chapter 3 just
for luck

The Evil Eye shall have no power to harm
Him that shall wear the diamond as a charm,
No monarch shall attempt to thwart his will,
And e'en the gods his wishes shall fulfil.

Orphic Poem

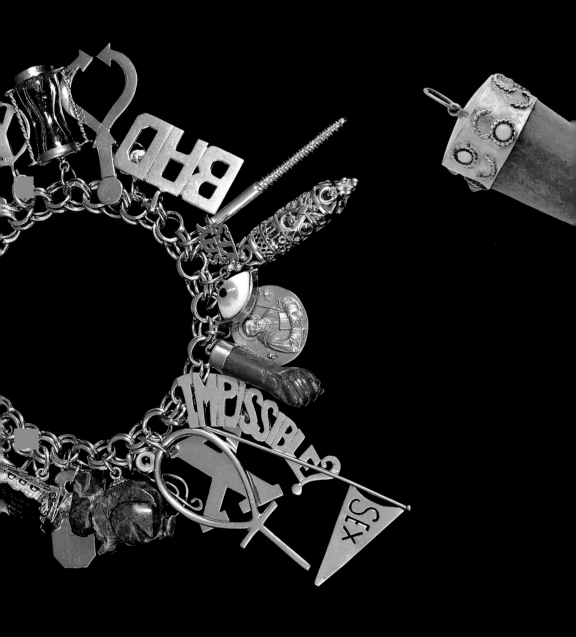

Our luck does not always lie in the lap of the gods. We have looked to the earth, too, to provide magical protection. Since records began, rare and precious stones have been mined for their powers. Lapidaries listing their marvellous properties date back to the Babylonians.

By combining a lucky symbol and a particular gemstone, a doubly effective charm can be made. In China it is believed that the power of the Buddha is enhanced if the statue is made of *jade*, a substance thought to be the most precious gift the Immortals have given to Man. Jade is often carried for luck in the Far East.

The equivalent in Italy is *coral*, which is worn for fertility, and is especially potent if in the form of a figa. Elizabeth Taylor carries an example of the *figa* amulet on a charm bracelet laden with attitude. In South America it is thought that if a woman sits on the thumb of a figa overnight she will conceive. Coral's association with children also makes it a popular amulet for the young. Queen Elizabeth II's first piece of jewelry was a coral necklace.

The ubiquitous horseshoe charm is used for good luck in both the East and West. The versatility of the form may play a part in its

widespread appeal. The U-shape is believed to trap the gaze of the Evil Eye; the crescent also embodies the symbol of the new moon; and, in addition, the curve can be interpreted as a 'C', incorporating Christian protection. Before the Battle of Trafalgar, Admiral Nelson attached a lucky *horseshoe* to the mast of his flagship HMS Victory, and the late Diana, Princess of Wales, alongside countless other brides, had a lucky horseshoe woven into her wedding dress. The symbol also makes for an attractive pendant on a simple chain, as worn by the actress Sarah Jessica Parker, and features amongst a plethora of charms engraved on a Dunhill lighter from the 1920s.

For the Ancients the natural world was the primary source of protective, magical or lucky charms. Prehistoric graves have been discovered containing, amongst their hoards of treasures, necklaces made of ornamented canine teeth, believed to have been worn with magical intention. Ancient flint arrowheads were set like teeth in Etruscan necklaces from Antiquity, and beads of paste or glass, known as serpent's eggs, have been found in Anglo-Saxon graves.

In Victorian England the tradition continued, with trophies from the animal kingdom, such as tiger claws, being mounted in jewelry. The belief in the power of the tiger to ward off evil had migrated across the British Empire from India.

Although belief in the magical power of jewels may have become diluted along the way, it was kept alive by the high priestess of sentiment, Queen Victoria, who owned countless charms. She even wore a bracelet made up of her children's first milk teeth. This is not quite as unusual as it sounds as, over a thousand years before, the Ancient Roman writer Pliny had observed that the first tooth lost by a child had magical properties. Indeed in the 1930s Fulco di Verdura succumbed to his client the Baronne Elie de Rothschild's penchant for sentimental jewelry, and designed for her a lily-of-the-valley spray made up of her children's milk teeth.

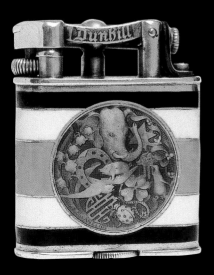

In Malta the fossilized teeth of sharks, known as St Paul's Tongue amulets, have offered particular protection against poisoning and general protection against the Evil Eye since medieval times. The name derives from St Paul's curse on the poisonous snakes of the island, one of whom bit him. When the snakes died, their tongues were thought to have been left in the rock, from which they were hewn to wear as amulets.

Toadstone, popular in the Middle Ages to cure dropsy and spleen, was actually made from the fossilized teeth of fish. It was also worn as a special protector of newborn children.

The unusual or inexplicable has always generated an air of mystery and magic. The horn of the unicorn – actually the horn of the narwhal – rare in appearance and difficult to find, was believed to contain magical properties that could detect poison in Tudor times – a real danger in the political maelstrom that was European courtlife at the time. *The Danny Jewel*, a wondrous creation of horn, was made in England and dates from the sixteenth century.

It is not just the rare and strange from the animal kingdom that historically provided lucky charms and symbols. As far back as the Babylonians, Man has looked heavenwards for protection. The word 'talisman' itself means some object to which the magical powers of the planetary influences under which it was made are attributed.

Cursory glances at horoscopes today belie the serious nature of the astrological beliefs that have come down the centuries. Signs of the Zodiac have been detected on an Egyptian tomb from the 4th century BC, and it is known that the Egyptians borrowed the Zodiac from the Greeks who, in turn, received its wisdom from the Babylonians.

Shining through the darkness we all share, stars are universal symbols of the spirit, and have long been looked up to as the dwelling place of the divine. A shooting star is commonly thought of as an augury of momentous happenings, and to be born under a *lucky star* is still cause for celebration. In traditions as varied as Islam and the Chukchee culture of Siberia, the Pole Star is a focal point. In Judaism the six-pointed Star of David, or Seal of Solomon, has an ancient history as a charm against evil and misfortune.

A deeply superstitious Coco Chanel is quoted as saying, 'I wanted to cover women in constellations. *Stars! Stars of all sizes*...' Countless jewelers have mined the form's possibilities in a range of stunning designs, from Cartier's white gold and diamond star to Chanel's shooting star, Theo Fennell's glamorous outline and Nigel Milne's vintage lucky star locket. As a good luck symbol, the star is one of the most enduring.

Every culture has its own particular tokens of good fortune, whether the lucky rabbit foot dangling from the rear-view mirror of an American car, the lucky cat placed in the window of a Japanese restaurant to welcome guests, or the lucky *four-leaf clover*, here interpreted by Chanel and Cartier.

Keys are also credited with magical powers, locking danger out, keeping prosperity in, symbolizing spiritual enlightenment and opening the door to exciting new stages of life. Like the owners of these multicoloured Theo Fennell charms, we all long to be blessed with the *keys to good fortune!*

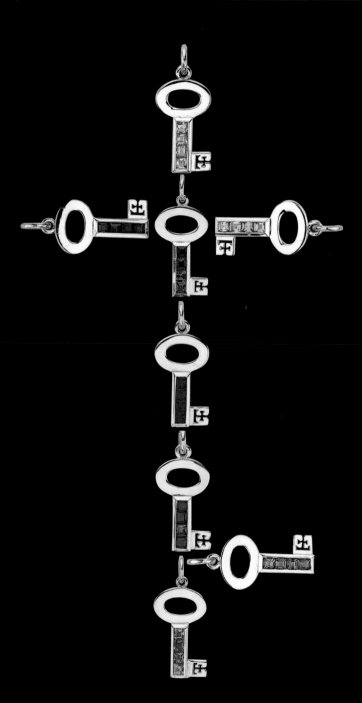

chapter 4 love tokens

Give me an amulet
That keeps intelligence with you,
Red when you love, and rosier red,
And when you love not, pale and blue.

Ralph Waldo Emerson, 'The Amulet'

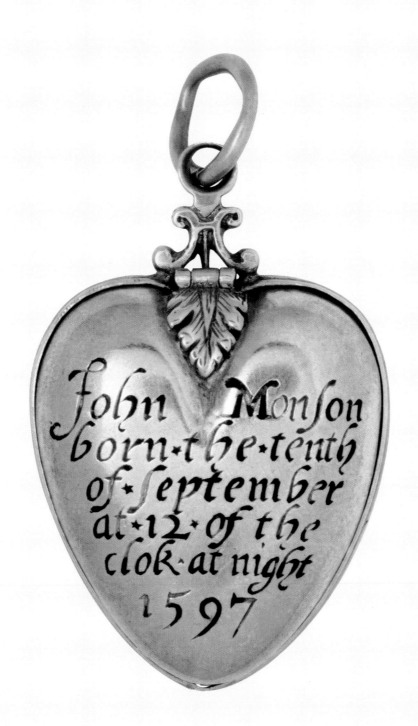

One of the most evocative and popular of all charms must be the heart. It provides constant reassurance through symbolizing belief in the protective power of love. Over four hundred years separates these three *gold heart charms* – a 'caul' locket to celebrate a birth in 1597, a chunky heart pendant from Links of London and an open heart by Elsa Peretti for Tiffany – but the sentiment they convey remains the same. A universal symbol of love, as well as a heraldic emblem of kindness and charity, the heart is the most enduring of charms.

Elizabeth Taylor's heart charm bracelet is a sentimental journey reflecting her love for her children, husbands, friends and pets.

For Joan Burstein, fashion doyenne and owner of the well-known London boutique Browns, her heart charm bracelet has become a treasure trove of all the loves and special occasions in her life.

The symbol of the heart crosses cultural and spiritual boundaries, and is as important in the East as in the West. In Islamic tradition, it represents the essence of the individual, the centre of contemplation and spiritual life, and sacred words from the Koran are sometimes added to it. Earlier hearts reflected a more accurate depiction of the actual organ. The familiar cleavage is a later development, thought to have stemmed from a shift to a more modern and Western interpretation of the heart.

If originally the heart was the symbol of life itself, we now view it as the embodiment of romantic or sentimental love. Mothers leaving their babies at the Foundling Hospital in London in the seventeenth century would often leave a *token in the shape of a heart* as a symbol of a continuing maternal presence as well as future protection.

This unusual *red heart* from the seventeenth century has fixed to it a lock of King Charles I's hair.

Contemporary jewelers, using the finest materials and exquisite craftsmanship, have succeeded in rising to the challenge of finding new expressions for this age-old symbol. Alluring takes on the heart form include Harry Winston's dazzling heart-shaped cut diamond and Chrome Hearts' Gothic heart in their signature black and silver finish.

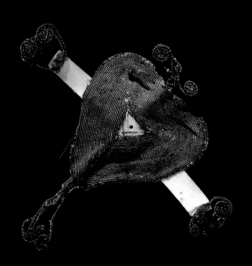

Another interpretation of the heart charm rediscovered by today's designers is the heart locket. This offers an alternative means of personalizing a love token. Such a keepsake might contain the image of a lover, or a lock of hair – something to remember the loved one by when apart.

In 1916 *Vogue* declared in its editorial: 'The *miniature* by appealing to the imagination still has the power to charm us by a sort of music – it can control our mood like a sonnet and it can be fanciful.' King George IV kept faith with his true love Maria Fitzherbert through such a miniature portrait. On his deathbed a locket depicting Mrs Fitzherbert and containing a lock of her hair was found beneath his nightshirt.

The same *Vogue* article went on to declare: 'War has brought back to favour that old-time token of sentiment, the silhouette portrait.' The height of fashion in the mid-eighteenth to early nineteenth centuries, silhouettes – worn as pendants or mounted on bracelet clasps – were the glamorous but affordable alternative to the painted miniature.

Another more unusual love charm,
particularly popular in the eighteenth
century, was the eye miniature. Here the eye
of a loved one is depicted and worn as a
continual *watchful presence*.

Hair was typically used in lockets and hidden
in charms as a love token, whether from the
living or the dead. This was taken to extremes
in the late Victorian fashion for hair jewelry,
whereby entire bracelets were made out of
the hair of a departed loved one.

On 14 December 1861, on the premature death of *her beloved* Prince Albert, Queen Victoria went into a deep mourning from which she would never recover. To ensure her husband's continued loving presence, she wore a bracelet with

his cameo on her wrist until the end of her days. She also had a cast of his hand laid like a protective charm on the pillow next to her every night.

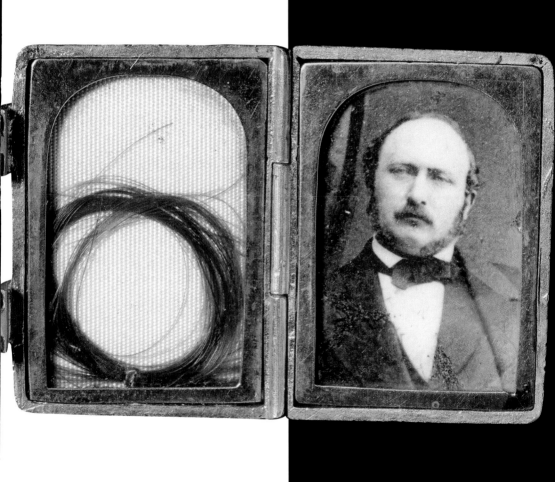

Stones themselves can convey a sentiment, and can thus be chosen for charms according to their own particular qualities. Sapphires are associated with wisdom, turquoise with healing, amethysts with romance, rubies with passion. The diamond, being the hardest and most enduring of stones, is associated with everlasting love. In China jade is regarded as the concentrated essence of love, and brides-to-be are often presented by their future husbands with jade butterflies.

In the nineteenth century it became fashionable to use the initial letters of the stones in a piece of jewelry to spell out a message of love. 'REGARD' was spelled out with a Ruby, Emerald, Garnet, Amethyst, Ruby and Diamond. This *language of sentiment* was still current in the twentieth century, as an American bracelet from 1935 shows. Each 'envelope' opens to reveal the photograph of a loved one, and the stones themselves – Diamond, Emerald, Amethyst, Ruby, Emerald, Sapphire and Tourmaline – spell out the endearment.

In the twenty-first century we are inventing
our own personalized languages of sentiment.
Meaning can be instilled in the most unusual
or whimsical of charms – a tiny cell phone
to remind us of a treasured friend, a polka
dot bikini to remember a holiday in the sun.
For those who wish their special memories to
have a further link to the past, vintage charms
may be sought out.

In order to commemorate his love affair with
Gloria Vanderbilt, Frank Sinatra presented
her with a dangling charm with a message:
'From miracle and me' spelled out in
diamonds. Vanderbilt later exclaimed, 'And
that's just how it was – a miracle coming at
exactly the right moment.'

But as well as being overt declarations of
love, charms by their delicate nature are
small enough to be worn covertly by those
who want, or need, to keep their love secret.

French was often used to express sentiment
in love tokens, as historically French was
the language of *courtly love*. This
1940s love token, with its inscription
'*pour vivre heureux, vivons cachés*' ('to live
happily, let us live hidden'), is clearly a gift
between secret lovers who had to remain
undiscovered, behind closed doors.

Lockets can be used to safeguard anything
precious. These miniature hearts, designed
by Links of London, are secret *romantic
tokens* of loved ones, important dates,
special moments, even weddings...

Other witty charms have used codes to communicate in secret. This tradition has been continued by the Scottish jewelry designer Eric Smith in his Morse Code diamond collection.

For King Edward VIII, charms had a more profound meaning. His *love affair with Wallis Simpson* was marked and celebrated in their own secret form of communication through charms. The couple, excluded from court, had to construct a world of their own, which was encapsulated in their personalized jewelry. In 1934 Edward gave Wallis a bracelet with a single cross on it. He was to add to it more crosses – tangible tokens of their love – over the next ten years. Edward, too, wore crosses, reciprocal gifts from Wallis.

The intimate personal experiences signified in charms tell a unique tale, a love story expressed through a very special language.

chapter 5
style and
sensibility

'In order to be irreplaceable
           one must always be different.'

Coco Chanel

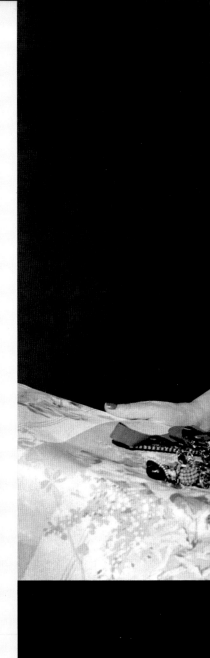

The iconic *Elizabeth I*, who gave her name to an era, was drawn to the whimsical nature of charms. A jewelry lover in all its forms, she reveled in the New Year's tradition of giving and receiving jewels as gifts. In 1587 she received charms in the shapes of a kettle, a warming pan and a frog (the pet name for her French suitor, the duc d'Alençon). Yet she also valued charms for their magical power, giving her favourite, the second Earl of Essex, a protective ring. Elizabeth herself favoured pearls, which, as symbols of purity, are particularly appropriate for the Virgin Queen.

In our own era charms have become a powerful
fashion statement as well as an eclectic
celebration of personal style. The queen of
cosmetics *Helena Rubinstein* was one
among many to be devoted to her collection
of charm jewelry.

A wrist jangling with charms is all about self-confidence and getting noticed. As jeweler Zahra Sajan says, 'Women like dangly things, and things that make noise or create attention.' Luminaries of the 1930s, such as *Joan Crawford* and Gloria Swanson, wore charm bracelets. Three decades later Sophia Loren and Jackie Kennedy Onassis were sporting them, too. And they are once again making an appearance on today's red carpets.

The forms that many modern charms now take have remained consistent with the forms of charms from previous centuries. Seals, for example, were popular with the Babylonians, Greeks and Romans, and then experienced a revival in the twentieth century, as attested by Elizabeth Taylor's gold charm bracelet with its sumptuous *intaglio seals*.

Coco Chanel put her inimitable style print on ancient charms by mixing her own brand of costume jewelry with ancestral gifts from her lover, the Grand Duke Dimitri of Russia. Charms of old coins were mixed with more modern Maltese crosses and seals. These charm bracelets and necklaces were a dramatic addition to her signature piece, the Little Black Dress – that staple of every stylish woman's wardrobe ever since.

Chanel also surrounded herself with her own *lucky motifs*. She adorned her creations with personal emblems such as the signature interlocking 'C's, the camellia and the lucky number 5.

reminiscent of her grandfather's watch chain. Schiaparelli's charm bracelets used gilt seals, intaglios and crystals, and even miniature vegetables – heirlooms of her Surrealist heritage.

Schiaparelli's style also drew on *astrological influences* Her uncle, an astronomer, made a link between a pattern of moles on her left cheek and the group of stars known as the Big Dipper, believed to impart wisdom, caution, versatility and power. The uncle pointed out that, far from being ugly, the moles and their particular configuration marked Elsa out as someone special. From that moment she adopted

Chanel and Schiaparelli's passion for charms finds echoes in twenty-first-century designers who are using their power to individualize garments and to weave a little magic into the fabric itself. As Alexander McQueen has said, 'You put a piece of yourself into it. You can't help it. That's what the customer gets, in a way – a piece of your emotion.'

Matthew Williamson is a devotee who often includes charms in his collections. These accessories add a *personal message*, whether for luck, love, hope or happiness.

Clements Ribeiro incorporate lucky motifs into their clothes. A four-leaf-clover print from their Spring/Summer 2004 collection lends a dress an *air of optimism*, the charm extending its protection to the wearer.

Charms are also adorning status bags from luxury brands including Mulberry and Prada, transforming them into one-off pieces and statements of individuality. Lulu Guinness decorates her handbags with personal motifs – a *Scottie dog* she longed to have, as well as glamorous feminine essentials such as a dressing table mirror and an evening shoe.

Other designers are coming up with interesting ways of expressing personal style. The jewelry designer Pippa Small draws on her anthropological studies to imbue her pieces with a talismanic significance.

At the Links of London 'charm bar', customers sit on bar stools, creating their own personal combinations of charms from a 'cocktail list' of hundreds of designs. This 'girlie, but glamorous' feeling in fashion is one of the keys to today's renaissance of charms.

chapter 6
milestones and celebrations

'If you are giving a jewel as a holiday gift,
make sure it is filled with charm.
Make that charms.'

Suzy Menkes

Charm collections are the perfect map of a full life lived. They record an individual's experiences, thereby creating an anthology of treasured moments – a landmark birthday reached, an exam passed with flying colours, the purchase of one's very first car...

Charms today are popular gifts to celebrate the arrival of a newborn. Since the 1950s, Aaron Basha has built a significant following in the United States for his enamel baby shoe charms, while Links of London's *baby charm* bracelets are hung with enchanting miniature totems such as shoes, baby carriages and toy animals.

When charms are exchanged between friends, even the most *fun and frivolous* become freighted with touching messages of love and camaraderie. Links of London's 'Foxy Lady' charm bracelet makes for a playful and witty way to celebrate a friendship – the high-heeled shoe for a shopaholic style diva, the martini glass to remember a great night out...

A popular way to commemorate engagements, weddings and anniversaries, charms can also be used to celebrate the lighter-hearted aspects of relationships. As a tongue-in-cheek gift, this saucy 'Can Can' bracelet makes for the perfect *indulgent treat*.

After the filming of *Charlie's Angels: Full Throttle*, the actress Demi Moore gave her co-star Lucy Liu a teddy bear and baby bottle charm. And on the birth of her daughter Apple, Gwyneth Paltrow commissioned from the jeweler Natasha Dahlberg a necklace and bracelet complete with distinctive apple charm. Such *sweet gestures* can equally be made from a parent to a child. Emerald Fennell, the daughter of jeweler Theo, has a charm bracelet hung with reminders of her best friends and her favourite things: the microphone for her love of entertainment, the guitar a testament to one of her great passions. The 'Music Man' vintage piece from Tiffany celebrates a similar enthusiasm.

The sheer variety of charm designs available means that each one of us can create a distinctive story according to our own interests and achievements, and the people we know and love. In *signature pieces*, fun and quirky charms are as appropriate as emotionally charged ones, and objets trouvés can take their place beside bespoke items.

Charms are building blocks for a myriad different life stories – no one the same. They can take the form of a solitaire ring to mark an engagement, sunglasses for a sun-worshipper, a watering can for the green-fingered, a lipstick for the glamorous, a treble clef for the musical, a karma sandal for the hippy.

This bracelet was assembled as a surprise birthday gift by a group of friends. Each charm has a particular meaning and celebrates the individual's special relationship with the birthday girl – the miniature cutlery set, for example, is a testament to a shared appreciation of gourmet cooking, the Prada bag a token of a mutual love of retail therapy, and the flipflop a reminder of great holidays in the South of France.

As well as remembering happy holidays, charms can be worn to commemorate a honeymoon or a year out. A little vintage Tiffany Cadillac and a Louis Vuitton charm bracelet in white gold celebrate the *romance of travel*. For every mini-adventure on your epic journey, a charm is left to tell the tale, to mark the moment.

Louis Vuitton's charms, first created by Marc Jacobs in 2002, include globes, aeroplanes, the company's cult monogram travel bags, the Citroën 2CV, the archetypal French car, the Eiffel Tower, that most celebrated landmark in the most famous *city of lovers*, and even spaceships as future emblems of the art of travel. These individual charms, like the Tiffany wagon, are designed to enable us to celebrate our own personal journeys.

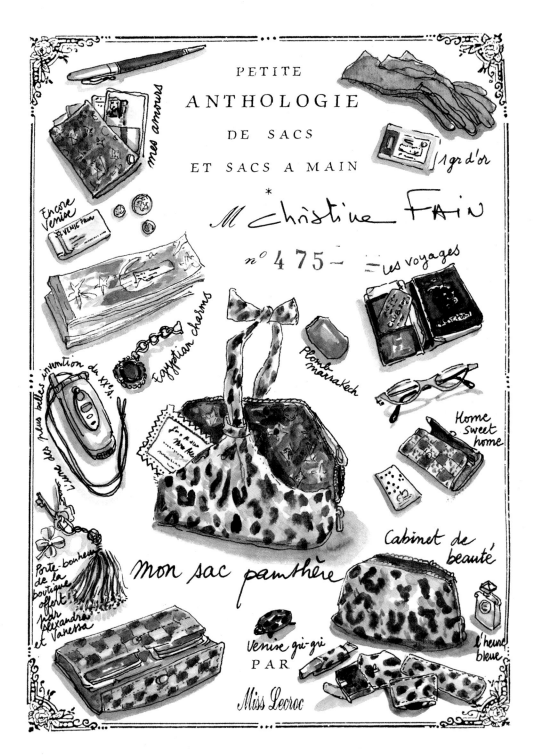

PETITE
ANTHOLOGIE
DE SACS
ET SACS A MAIN

Another, more quirky, record of a journey through life is held in a woman's handbag. Nathalie Lecroc, a Parisian artist, paints portraits by exploring the contents of her sitters' bags. She has discovered that many women carry with them a lucky charm or coin, a friendly presence to keep the owner safe. As Mlle Lecroc observes, 'French women are obsessed with *lucky mascots.*'

Charms are fun and there to be enjoyed, but they can also be *treasures to be stored up* for future generations. Because of their intimate nature, they carry with them a sense of the giver. When such an heirloom is passed on, part of the personality of the giver is passed on with it, acting as a continued loving or protective presence.

This is the story of charms. It is a story bound up with the universal themes of love, luck and protection. What this story shows is the enduring nature of these themes. We, in a new millennium, are enjoying the same magic of charms as our forebears thousands of years ago.

list of illustrations